A Note to Parents

DK READERS is a compelling program for beginning readers, designed in conjunction with leading literacy experts, including Dr. Linda Gambrell, Distinguished Professor of Education at Clemson University. Dr. Gambrell has served as President of the National Reading Conference and the College Reading Association, and is President of the International Reading Association.

Beautiful illustrations and superb full-color photographs combine with engaging, easy-to-read stories to offer a fresh approach to each subject in the series. Each DK READER is guaranteed to capture a child's interest while developing his or her reading skills, general knowledge, and love of reading.

The five levels of DK READERS are aimed at different reading abilities, enabling you to choose the books that are exactly right for your child:

Pre-level 1: Learning to read
Level 1: Beginning to read
Level 2: Beginning to read alone
Level 3: Reading alone
Level 4: Proficient readers

The "normal" age at which a child begins to read can be anywhere from three to eight years old. Adult participation through the lower levels is very helpful for providing encouragement, discussing storylines, and sounding out unfamiliar words.

No matter which level you select, you can be sure that you are helping your child learn to read, then read to learn!

LONDON, NEW YORK, MUNICH,
MELBOURNE, AND DELHI

Publisher Beth Sutinis
Editor Brian Saliba
Custom Publishing Director Mike Vacarro
Managing Art Director Michelle Baxter

Reading Consultant
Linda Gambrell, Ph.D.

Produced by
Shoreline Publishing Group LLC
President James Buckley, Jr.
Designer Tom Carling, carlingdesign.com

The Boy Scouts of America®, Cub Scouts®,
Boys' Life®, and rank insignia are registered
trademarks of the Boy Scouts of America.
Printed under license from the
Boy Scouts of America.

First American Edition, 2007
07 08 09 10 11 10 9 8 7 6 5 4 3 2 1
Published in the United States by DK Publishing
375 Hudson Street, New York, New York 10014

Copyright © 2007 Dorling Kindersley Limited

Published in Great Britain by Dorling Kindersley Limited

DK books are available at special discounts when purchased in bulk
for sales promotions, premiums, fund-raising, or educational use.
For details, contact:
DK Publishing Special Markets, 375 Hudson St., New York, NY 10014
SpecialSales@dk.com

A catalog record for this book is available
from the Library of Congress.
ISBN: 978-0756-635084 (Paperback)
ISBN: 978-0756-635091 (Hardcover)

Printed and bound in Mexico by R.R. Donnelley.

The publisher would like to thank the following for their kind
permission to reproduce their photographs:
(Key: a=above; b=below/bottom; c=center; l=left; r=right; t=top)
Courtesy American Honda: 40; AP/Wide World: 13; Art Archive/Victoria and Albert Museum/Sally
Chappell: 8; Corbis: 35, 39; Courtesy of the Department of Cybernetics, University of Reading: 38;
Intuitive Surgical, Inc.: 28, 30, 31; iStock: 5, 24, 33; Todd Jacobs/NOAA: 25; Mary Evans Picture
Library: 11; Courtesy of the National Environment Research Council and Nick Millard of the
Southampton Oceanography Centre: 26; NASA: 14, 16, 17, 19; Photos.com: 7; Courtesy John Rigg,
The Robot Hut: 9, 37, 44; Courtesy of Peter Rowe and Dave Pearson of Kawazaki Robotics Ltd.: 21;
Science and Society Picture Library: 12; Tokyo Institute of Technology: 24; University of
Southampton: 32; Volker Steger/Photo Researchers: 25. All other images © Dorling Kindersley
Limited.For more information see: www.dkimages.com

Discover more at
www.dk.com

Contents

Boys' Life SERIES
Real-Life
Robots

Written by James Buckley Jr.

DK Publishing

Here come the robots!

The giant, clanking metal creature stomps into view. People panic in the streets. Cars race away from the danger. Soldiers prepare to defend the city. What's going on?

A huge robot is attacking! Its long arms and enormous feet smash through the city's buildings. Its human-like hand reaches down, picks up an empty truck and crushes it like a grape. It moves its head from side to side, its lighted eyes looking ahead to watch for obstacles. Like a giant metal person, the robot storms forward. Can anyone stop it?!

And then . . . the TV show cuts to a commercial. It's a good thing this is only a TV show! Robots can't really walk around, can they? They can't pick things up, right? Robots can't possibly be real, can they?

Well, robots can't attack cities (yet!), but robots are definitely real!

Robots only attack cities in science fiction stories. For more than 50 years, robots of all shapes and sizes have been helping human beings in many ways.

Real-life robots dive beneath the ocean waves, help doctors do surgery, or keep soldiers safe. Other robots work in factories to help build cars and other products. And some robots are just fun toys to play with!

But what is a robot? That's actually a tricky question. Different experts on robots will give you different answers. But the easy way to think of a robot is this: A machine that can move around or do different activities without direct help from a person. Computers aren't robots because computers can't move. Other machines are just remote controlled and can't move on their own.

While TV and movie robots often look like people, most of today's real-life robots don't. Let's take a look at the many ways that robots are a big part of the world today.

Robots can be powerful . . . and sensitive.

History of robots

The idea of making machines that could act like people or animals has been around for a long time. Ancient Greeks made birds that "flew" by themselves. Chinese artists made dolls that "served" tea to guests. The dolls used springs and gears to move. A musical organ made in India moved when played—it looked like a tiger attacking a soldier! But these devices were mostly toys or simple gadgets.

A musical Indian toy

Real robots were still in the future.

The period of history called the Industrial Revolution helped spread the idea of robots. This period, during the late 1800s, saw the invention of many new machines. Steam power drove some of them, while the use of electricity was

Oz's Tin Man

increasing. The idea that a human-like machine could be made to replace people became popular in stories. The Tin Man and Tik-Tak characters from the *Wizard of Oz* were mechanical men, or robots, for instance.

Inventors and scientists started trying to use the power of machines to make more complicated human-like machines. For example, inventor Louis Perew's Automatic Man walked and pulled a cart in 1900. Finally, in 1920, the word "robot" was first used. It debuted not in a laboratory or a factory . . . but in a play! Author Karel Capek wrote a play called "Rossum's Universal Robots." The word "robot" came from *robota* in the Czech [CHECK] language. In Czech, the word means "hard work."

Capek's robots inspired many artists and builders. Kids were the first to enjoy robots—toy robots, that is. However, these toys did not work as real robots. They could not move by themselves or perform tasks (or take over cities!).

The toys—often made from metal—were designed to be what people imagined robots would one day look like.

However, with the spread of computers in the years following World War II (1939-1945), technology met imagination. Finally, robots became real!

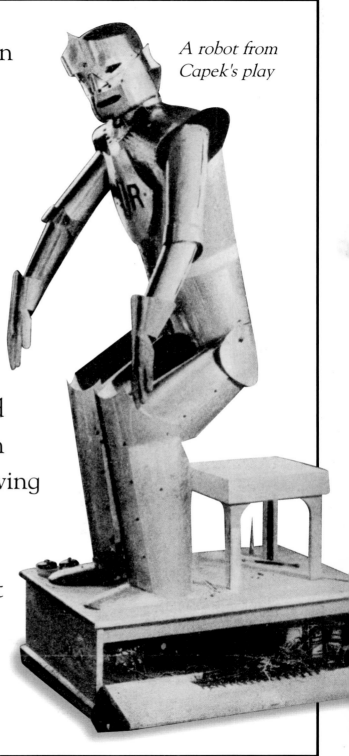

A robot from Capek's play

With computers, scientists could give their robot machines a "brain." In 1948, Grey Walter put such a brain inside a low, round, plastic shell on wheels. Because of the shape, he called his creations "tortoises." With help from a controller's radio, they could roll on their own and sense their surroundings.

Walter's 1948 "tortoise" robot

The Three Laws

Isaac Asimov was a famous science fiction writer. His imagination led scientists to see if they could create what he put in his stories. In 1941, he wrote  the "Three Laws of Robotics. These laws were designed to prevent robots from becoming more powerful than humans. Asimov's Three Laws: 1. A robot may not injure a human being. 2. A robot must obey orders given to it by a human, except where those orders would break the first law. 3. A robot must try to "stay alive," except where that would break either of the other laws.

Robots and computers became smarter and more complicated. In 1962, the first robot was used in a factory. It could repeat a task endlessly without getting tired—or making a mistake. In 1966, a robot called "Shakey" was the first to move freely and without help.

Since those early days, the science of "robotics" has grown and grown.

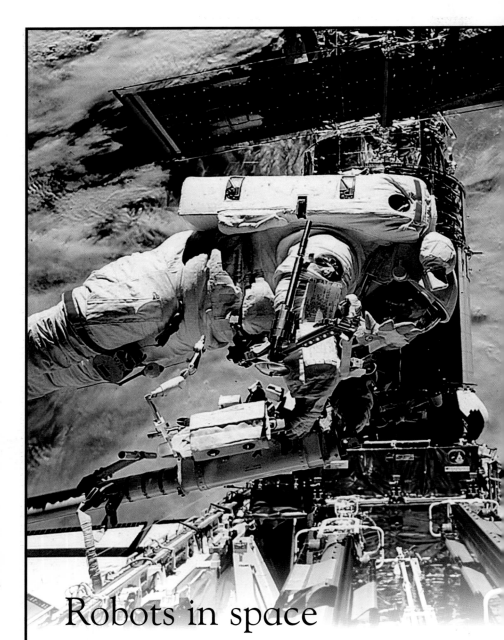

Robots in space

When people go into space, they
need spacesuits, oxygen, food, water,
and other survival gear. Space can be

a dangerous place for people to work. However, robots don't need any of that. They are safe without air or water. They can work around the clock, too—robots don't need to sleep! So robots play a big part in the exploration of space.

The simplest robot used in space is the robot arm of the International Space Station. It can move steadily to help spacewalkers or to carry gear outside the station. The space shuttle also has a mechanical arm to assist astronauts.

NASA has also created the multi-purpose Robonaut, which might someday go into space to assist astronauts with space station repairs.

Robot arm lifts satellite

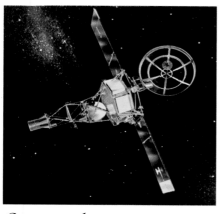
Space probe

Some robots roam among the stars exploring space. Space agencies from countries around the world have launched probes, or machines that capture information about space. These probes zoom through the solar system. Some have even left the solar system to explore distant space objects such as comets or asteroid belts.

The probes are like robots because they have to work for long periods without getting instructions from a person. They automatically get their energy through solar batteries. They take pictures and beam information back to Earth. They measure distances and examine anything they can "see" on their long journeys.

NASA has sent such probes to all the planets in the solar system. These probes have given us amazing views of places we can't see even with the strongest telescopes.

Viking
Mars probe

Other independent machines in space take the place of astronauts on far-away worlds. No human being has ever visited Mars, but several robots have! The first was called *Sojourner*. It landed on Mars in 1997. For three months, it rolled around the surface, sending back pictures and data.

This Russian rover was the first to land on the Moon.

The Mars rover Spirit *moves around on six wheels.*

In 2003, two more rovers, named *Spirit* and *Opportunity*, landed on Mars. Scientists thought these machines would stop working in a few months. However, more than four years later, the two were still chugging along, sending back information about the harsh world of Mars. Only a robot could do this work so well and for so long in a place so unfriendly to humans.

Robots at work

Back on Earth, robots make many people's jobs easier and safer. Because robots can work for long periods without resting,

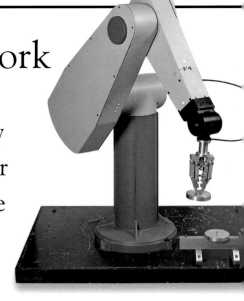

Unimate

they can do more work. Factories can be open more hours and make more of their products, thanks to robots.

More than a million robots work building cars, trucks, and other large machines. The first factory robot, called Unimate, was built

Design for robot arm

in 1962. Since then, robots have moved into factories around the world. Most are very simple and do just one thing. They often look like a giant arm, with an "elbow" and "wrist." Bolted in one place, the arm repeats its movements over and over as cars roll by on an assembly line. Some robots attach parts, some weld parts together, others lift heavy objects for people to work on. Human workers have to program, or give directions to, factory robots, but once the robots are turned on, no one has to tell them what to do.

A modern factory arm

Robots also help keep people safe. Police officers control special types of robots that can disarm bombs or other explosives. The cameras on the rolling robots let the officers see the danger from a safe distance away.

Firefighters can send in a robot to help control a fire in a place that would be too dangerous for a person. These types of robots can carry fire extinguishers or other things to help put out the fire. The firefighters direct the robots by watching video from the

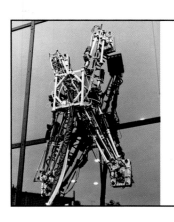

Cleaning robots
Cleaning windows on skyscrapers can be dangerous. In Japan, the "Ninja" robot was made to climb the outside of buildings. The Ninjas climb the windows, cleaning as they go.

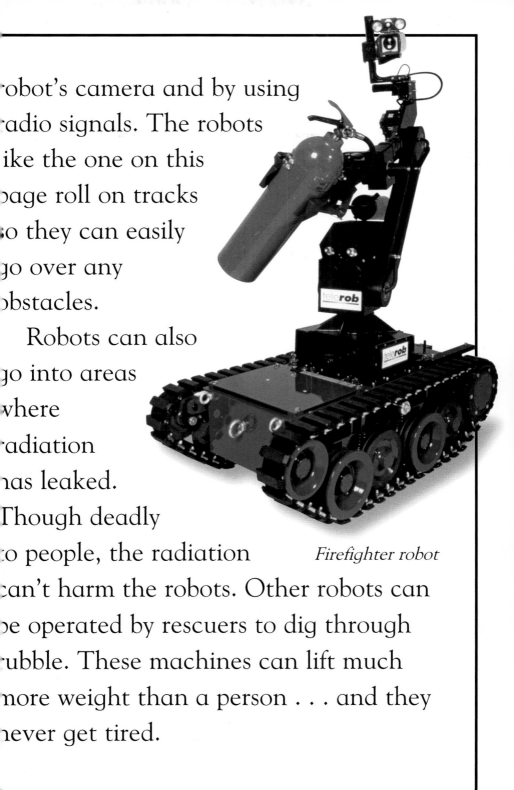

obot's camera and by using
adio signals. The robots
ike the one on this
page roll on tracks
o they can easily
go over any
obstacles.

Robots can also
go into areas
where
radiation
has leaked.
Though deadly
o people, the radiation

Firefighter robot

can't harm the robots. Other robots can
be operated by rescuers to dig through
rubble. These machines can lift much
more weight than a person . . . and they
never get tired.

Bomb-defusing robot

Sergeant Robot? Well, no, they don't have ranks, but robots are hard at work in the military. As in police work, robots are used to defuse bombs or go into areas that would be too dangerous for people. Some military robots act as security guards, patrolling to look for intruders. Robots are also used to clear minefields of dangerous explosives.

Most military robots are in the air,

however. Unmanned robotic aircraft are used in many ways by the armed forces. These robotic planes can fly over an area to take pictures or video to let soldiers know what's up ahead. Other planes are sent into enemy territory to spy without any harm coming to pilots.

Unmanned aircraft are also used by scientists. These robotic planes can track whales in the ocean, study weather patterns, or look for changes in ocean currents.

Unmanned research plane

You might think that a metal robot wouldn't do too well if it got wet. However, many robots are used underwater. Some are guided from the surface by remote control or through the use of long cables. Others roam around freely, much like robot space probes, sending back pictures and information. Some manned submarines have robot arms that are used to pick up objects from the seafloor.

Scientists in England developed a robot that looked like a shark. Filled with cameras, it could swim along with sharks and film

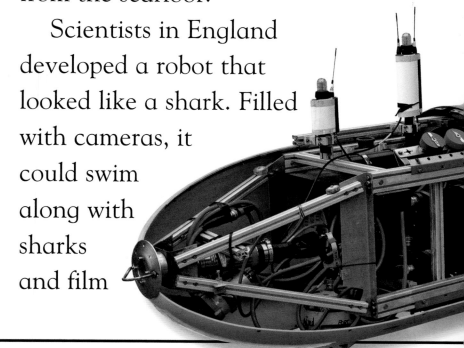

their behavior—
and fit right in!
Other
robot subs
search for

Cable-directed submersible

shipwrecks and help discover new sea
creatures. The best thing about using
these robots is that they can dive more
deeply than humans can. This means
scientists can explore many strange
new parts of the ocean—with help from
robots.

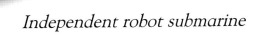

Independent robot submarine

Medical robots

A surgeon sits in New York City and operates on a patient. However, the patient is in France! How can that be? The answer can be found in robotics. Using a special machine linked to a robot, a surgeon can now operate via remote control. Cameras in the operating room give a close-up view of the patient. The surgeon uses a control pad to send commands to robot arms that do the actual surgery. This

28

obot lets skilled surgeons help people
around the world.

Another surgical robot is used in
brain surgeries. It can very precisely
place instruments and hold them
steady for long periods.

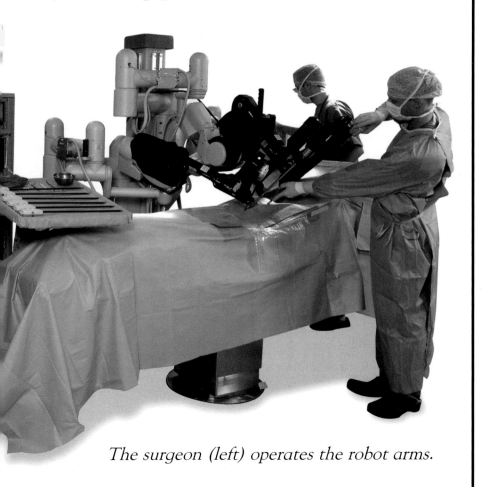

The surgeon (left) operates the robot arms.

Other robots are used when the surgeon is in the same room. The well-known DaVinci machine helps surgeons do operations on very tiny parts of the

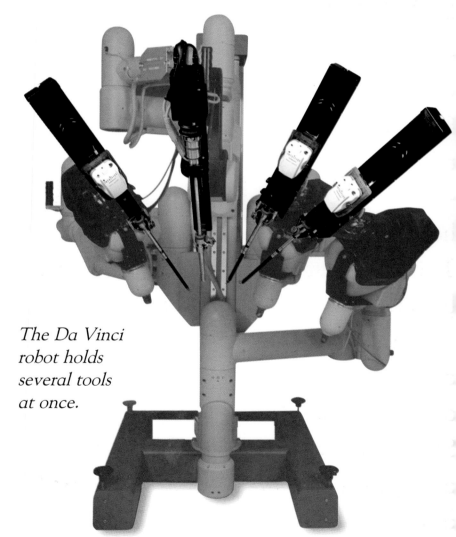

The Da Vinci robot holds several tools at once.

human body. Its tiny clips, or "fingers," can make very small movements that would be impossible for a person. Also, the robots can reduce the size of the cuts a surgeon has to make in the person.

Surgical robot camera

This can make the operation safer and help the patient recover faster.

Some hospitals use a robot called a Helpmate. It travels through hallways delivering files, X-rays, and records. Special sensors help it find its way around without hitting anyone or anything.

Have you ever heard of the Bionic Man? He was a character on a TV show in the 1970s. Supposedly, he was a pilot who was badly injured in an accident. Scientists "rebuilt" him with special robot parts that made him, as the show said, "better, stronger, faster." In reality, such "bionic" replacement parts for humans are a long way off. However, the science of robotics has helped people who lose limbs. Today, replacement hands, feet, and fingers are often like mini-robots. Using batteries and robotic

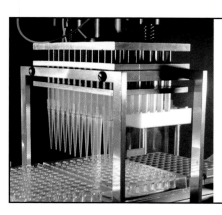

Medicine makers
Robots are used to make medicine. Creating medicines is very precise work. A mistake could be deadly. Robots can make perfect measurements.

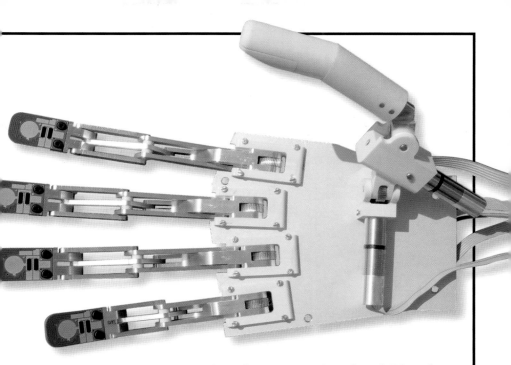

Southampton Artificial Hand

connections to the body, these new parts can act much as real body parts do.

For example, scientists in England created the Southampton Artificial Hand. They hope that its combination of computers, robotics, and sensors will help people who have lost a hand. With this hand, people might regain the ability to pick up objects or control things better than older types of artificial hands.

Having fun with robots

The life of a robot doesn't sound like too much fun so far. A robot explodes bombs, works 24 hours a day, or sticks its fingers into people's guts. Well, life is not all hard work for some robots. Creative inventors have used robotic technology to have all sorts of fun—and provide some for you, too.

The first robotic toys, of course, didn't really do anything. They looked like

Toy robot

obots from stories, but they didn't act ike them. Kids who played with them used their imagination to make the toys move or "talk." Many toys were based on robots from TV and the movies.

Today's robotic toys, however, can alk, walk, stand, pick up objects, and even dance—all by themselves! In 1998, the bubble-eyed Furby was one of the first interactive toys. That means it could respond to voice commands from its owner to speak or open its eyes.

Spot the robot?
The first robotic dog was exhibited in 1939 at the World's Fair in New York. He was the "pet" of a robot on display. The dog, named Sparko, could be made to sit up and look at its "master."

In 1999, Sony made AIBO (EYE-boh), a pet dog robot. AIBO was the first of many toy robots programmed to "act" like real pets or animals. The toys come with sensors to hear commands, voiceboxes to respond to the user, and sometimes even cameras to help them "see" and move around.

AIBO toy robo

A *toy "factory" robot*

Another popular type of toy robot comes in a kit. Users get all the parts of a robot and have the fun of making it themselves. Then they can turn it on and "program" it or operate it to do different things. The toy at the top here was made from a kit.

The newest toy robots are almost human in their apperance. They can dance to music, pick up objects, or walk around a room. Kids can choose how their toy robots move and make them "come to life."

Programmable toy robot

A BattleBot

Fun is, well . . . fun. But robots also can compete! Scientists studying robots use sports to test how well they're building their robots. For example, on a popular TV show called "BattleBots," two robots did their best to destroy each other while rolling around a small arena. The last robot running won.

Other scientists build robots that can play soccer. The annual Robot Soccer World Cup brings together amazing creations that can move around, kick a ball, and shoot. (They don't jump into each others' arms after they score, however!)

The RoboCup project is trying to build robots that are so human-like they can play soccer against people. Their goal is to beat the real World Cup champs by 2050.

Another competition is run by the U.S. government. The Defense Research Agency will pay $1 million to any team that can build a vehicle that drives from Los Angeles to Las Vegas . . . by itself.

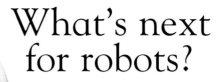

What's next for robots?

The years of advances in robotics are all leading to one thing: a true robot that looks and acts like a human. Several companies, mostly in Japan, are working hard to create the ultimate robot.

The impressive ASIMO robot can climb stairs and walk down hallways without human guidance. A backpack holds a large computer that powers ASIMO. This very human-looking robot, made by Honda, has appeared around the world, amazing viewers with its abilities. It can even shake hands!

The HOAP robots made by Fujitsu have arms and legs like people, but they can move in many ways that people can't. Users can even program it to do martial arts moves.

The friendly-looking Sony QRIO (pronounced "curio") robot can kick a ball, surf the Web, and even recognize your face. Turn on the right kind of music, and QRIO will dance.

The Sico Millennia robot is used on TV so often that is a member of an actor's union!

Sico Millennia

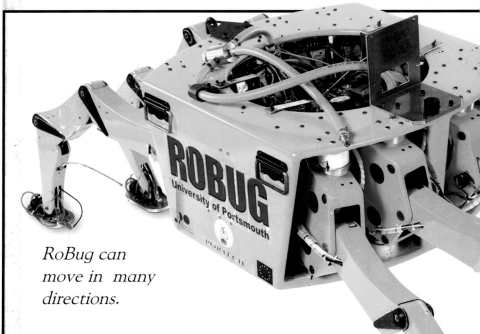

RoBug can move in many directions.

Thanks to the imagination of writers and the creative genius of scientists, robots are becoming more and more useful and human-like. We're still a long way from walking, talking androids like you see in famous science fiction movies. But robots are getting smarter and smarter. In the future, they will run trains, help us explore new worlds (or parts of our own world), and save lives.

How important are robots? They even have their own Hall of Fame now. At Carnegie Mellon University in Pennysylvania, scientists choose new members of the Robot Hall of Fame each year. They choose from both fiction and science. The lists on the next page let you meet these amazing robots. Keep an eye on the science pages and watch for more new robots coming into use around the world. Who knows? You might even build one of them yourself.

Mini-robot

Robot Hall of Fame Members:

Real Life

- AIBO: the popular toy dog
- ASIMO: Honda's walking robot
- Lego® Mindstorms: toys
- Mars Pathfinder *Sojurner*: space rover
- Navlab 5: robot car
- SCARA: a robot arm used to build electronics
- Shakey: the first robot that could direct its own movements
- 3D One-Leg Hopper/Biped/Quadriped: Three stages of robot evolution
- Unimate: first robot used in a factory

Gort

Fiction/Fantasy

Maria

- Astro Boy: Japanese TV cartoon first shown in 1951
- C-3PO: the talkative android from *Star Wars*
- Data: *Star Trek* android
- David: from the 2001 movie *A.I.: Artificial Intelligence*
- Gort: alien robot from 1951 movie *The Day the Earth Stood Still*
- HAL 9000: from the movie *2001: A Space Odyssey*
- Maria: from the 1927 movie *Metropolis*
- R2-D2: the little *Star Wars* android
- Robby the Robot: from the 1956 movie *Forbidden Planet*

Find out more

Here are some other books you can enjoy to learn more about robots, including how they are designed and built and what they do.

Eyewitness Robot
By Roger Bridgman
(DK, 2004)
Tons of photos of robots from science and science fiction are featured in this book. Meet the scientists who create real-life robots and learn what they've got planned for the future.

Ultimate Robot
(DK Publishing, 2004)
By Robert Malone
Written by a world-famous robot expert, this book has dozens of huge pictures of robots. It has an entire section on robots in art and entertainment. It also discusses robot kits that kids can use to build their own robots.

The Robot Kit
By Sarah Chapman
(Barron's, 2004)
This book-plus-kit includes everything you need (except batteries!) to build four small robots.

Robozones (Series)
By David Jefferis
(Crabtree, 2006)
This four-book series includes titles on Brains, Workers, Warriors, and Voyagers. Each takes a close-up look at real-life robots in those areas.

Here are some Web sites that you can visit to learn even more:

Robot Hall of Fame
www.robothalloffame.org
Meet the greatest robots of all time—both real and fictional. From movie stars to factory workers, the members of the Robot Hall of Fame all have interesting stories to tell about their part in the robotic world.

Real robot fans
www.robots.org
This site is run by the San Francisco Robotics Society of America. This is a private group made up of robot fans and scientists. The site offers link to other robot sites, projects you can try, and news from the world of real-life robots.

Help for school projects
www.robotics.com
Run by the Arrick Robotics Company, this site includes ideas on how to build a robot, news of latest advances in robotics, and a section that can help you do research for a school report or project.

Glossary

Android
A human-like machine that can think for itself.

Assembly line
A way of building products in a factory in which the product moves along a conveyor belt and parts are added one at a time.

Bionic
Combining living tissue and electronics.

Complicated
Very difficult, with many parts or ways of working.

Defuse
To make a bomb or landmine safe and unable to explode.

Gadget
A device, usually a small one, that performs a task in a new and interesting way.

Gravity
The force that holds all objects to the earth.

Guidance
Information or instructions provided to help a person or a machine complete a task.

Industrial
Having to do with powered machines used in factories.

Interactive
Responding to human commands.

Mechanical
Having to do with machines.

Probes
Unmanned machines sent into space to explore faraway places.

Radiation
Powerful, invisible energy waves given off by minerals and living things.

Robot
A machine that operates without direct human control and can move in several directions.

Robotics
The science of studying and building robots.

Rubble
Broken parts of buildings or other material left over a disaster of some sort.

Sensors
Devices that let a robot "feel" or "see" its environment.

Sojourner
The name of a space probe launched by NASA to explore Mars. The word means "traveler."

Submersible
A machine that goes underwater.

Surgeon
A doctor who works by cutting into a patient to repair damage due to illness or injury.

Index